99 Asthma Meal and Juice Recipes:

Naturally Reduce Chronic and Troublesome Symptoms

By

Joe Correa CSN

COPYRIGHT

© 2019 Live Stronger Faster Inc.

All rights reserved

Reproduction or translation of any part of this work beyond that permitted by section 107 or 108 of the 1976 United States Copyright Act without the permission of the copyright owner is unlawful.

This publication is designed to provide accurate and authoritative information in regard to the subject matter covered. It is sold with the understanding that neither the author nor the publisher is engaged in rendering medical advice. If medical advice or assistance is needed, consult with a doctor. This book is considered a guide and should not be used in any way detrimental to your health. Consult with a physician before starting this nutritional plan to make sure it's right for you.

ACKNOWLEDGEMENTS

This book is dedicated to my friends and family that have had mild or serious illnesses so that you may find a solution and make the necessary changes in your life.

99 Asthma Meal and Juice Recipes:

Naturally Reduce Chronic and Troublesome Symptoms

By

Joe Correa CSN

CONTENTS

Copyright

Acknowledgements

About The Author

Introduction

Commitment

99 Asthma Meal and Juice Recipes: Naturally Reduce Chronic and Troublesome Symptoms

Additional Titles from This Author

ABOUT THE AUTHOR

After years of Research, I honestly believe in the positive effects that proper nutrition can have over the body and mind. My knowledge and experience has helped me live healthier throughout the years and which I have shared with family and friends. The more you know about eating and drinking healthier, the sooner you will want to change your life and eating habits.

Nutrition is a key part in the process of being healthy and living longer so get started today. The first step is the most important and the most significant.

INTRODUCTION

99 Asthma Meal and Juice Recipes: Naturally Reduce Chronic and Troublesome Symptoms

By Joe Correa CSN

Asthma symptoms can be treated with certain foods that will prevent this disease, as well as improve your overall health. A healthy, nutrient-rich diet and regular exercise are some basic, general guidelines for a long and healthy life. In most cases, asthma is associated with obesity. This is why it's extremely important to control your body weight.

Most doctors agree that certain foods could also be triggers for asthma. If you notice an allergic reaction to some foods, you should consider avoiding them because these can be high-risk foods for your asthmatic condition.

On the other hand, there is one general rule for asthmatics, the less you eat fresh fruits and vegetables, the higher the frequency of asthma. As simple as that! That's why I want to give you a quick and tasty solution to your problem. I've made a collection of delicious recipes that will help treat and prevent asthma. These recipes are full of healthy nutrients, vitamins, minerals, omega-3 fatty acids and are delicious. They are full of fruits and vegetables, which have natural antioxidants that will help your body defeat the inflammatory process you're going through and protect your cells from any future problematic conditions.

Avoiding these common triggers will significantly reduce the risk of asthma. Furthermore, there are certain types of foods that are proven to help prevent and treat people diagnosed with asthma. Vitamin D rich foods like milk and eggs are often prescribed to patients suffering from asthma. Also, vegetables rich in beta-carotene such as carrots, bell peppers, pumpkin, and leafy greens are proven to be extremely beneficial for reducing the risk of asthma. Furthermore, some studies suggest that people with low magnesium levels have low lung volume. Adding foods rich in magnesium into your diet is an excellent way to prevent and treat asthma attacks.

This book contains asthma preventing juice recipes based on these particular foods that will help you reduce the risk of getting asthma in the first place. The juices in this book are very easy to make, healthy, and above all, delicious.

COMMITMENT

In order to improve my condition, I *(your name)*, commit to eating more of these foods on a daily basis and to exercise at least 30 minutes daily:

- Berries (especially blueberries), peaches, cherries, apples, apricots, oranges, lemon juice, grapefruit, tangerines, mandarins, pears, etc.
- Broccoli, spinach, collard greens, sweet potatoes, avocado, artichoke, baby corn, carrots, celery, cauliflower, onions, etc.
- Whole grains, steel-cut oats, oatmeal, quinoa, barley, etc.
- Black beans, red bean beans, garbanzo beans, lentils, etc.
- Nuts and seeds including: walnuts, cashews, flaxseeds, sesame seeds, etc.
- Fish
- 8 – 10 glasses of water

Sign here

X_____

99 ASTHMA MEAL AND JUICE RECIPES: NATURALLY REDUCE CHRONIC AND TROUBLESOME SYMPTOMS

MEAL RECIPES

1. Salmon & Veggies

Ingredients:

1 lb of wild salmon fillets, skinless and boneless

1 cup of white rice, long grain

1 cup of chicken broth

1 small zucchini, peeled and sliced

2 small carrots, sliced

1 tbsp of olive oil

¼ cup of lemon juice

1 tsp of fresh rosemary, finely chopped

¼ tsp of black pepper, ground

¼ tsp of sea salt

Preparation:

Preheat the oven to 375°F.

Combine salmon, lemon juice, rosemary, olive oil, salt, and pepper in a glass bowl. Coat well the meat and refrigerate 30 minutes before grilling.

Combine the rice and chicken broth to a medium pot over a medium-high temperature. Add carrots, zucchini, and sprinkle with some salt and pepper to taste. Bring it to a boil and remove from the heat. Set aside.

Place the salmon fillets in a large baking sheet over a piece of baking paper. Coat the fillets with rice and veggies mixture. Cover with aluminum foil and put it in the oven. Bake for about 10-15 minutes or until set. Serve warm.

Nutrition information per serving: Kcal: 347, Protein: 28.4g, Carbs: 28.3g, Fats: 17.6g

2. Cucumber Mint Smoothie

Ingredients:

1 large cucumber, chopped

1 cup of spinach, pre-cooked

1 tbsp of honey

¼ cup of mint leaves

1 cup of Greek yogurt

1 tbsp of lemon juice

1 tbsp of chia seeds

Preparation:

Place spinach in a pot of boiling water. Cook for 10 minutes or until soften. Drain and set aside to cool completely.

Now, combine spinach and all other ingredients in a blender. Blend until smooth and transfer to a serving glass.

Garnish with some fresh mint leaves and refrigerate for 30 minutes before serving.

Nutrition information per serving: Kcal: 130, Protein: 3.8g, Carbs: 31.6g, Fats: 0.7g

3. Gouda Onion Omelet

Ingredients:

4 free-range egg whites

1 free-range egg

3 tbsp of Gouda cheese, shredded

1 tbsp of skim milk

1 small onion, sliced

2 tsp of grapeseed oil

1 tsp of Dijon mustard

2 tbsp of white quinoa, pre-cooked

Preparation:

Pour one cup of water into a small pot and bring it to a boil. Spoon in the quinoa and cook for 15minutes. Remove from the heat and set aside to cool.

Meanwhile, preheat 1 tablespoon of grapeseed oil in a large saucepan over a medium-low temperature. Add the onion and a 1 tablespoon of water. Cover with a lid and cook until translucent. Remove from the heat and add mustard. Stir well to combine. Set aside.

Preheat another tablespoon of grapeseed oil in a large saucepan over a medium-low temperature. whisk the egg and egg whites in a mixing bowl. Add milk and pour the mixture into the saucepan. Cook for about 4-5 minutes from both sides. Spread the previously prepared quinoa and onions over one half and fold the omelet.

Sprinkle with shredded gouda and salt to taste.

Nutrition information per serving: Kcal: 210, Protein: 14.3g, Carbs: 18.5g, Fats: 8.6g

4. Ziti Casserole

Ingredients:

4 oz of ziti pasta

6 oz of ricotta cheese, crumbled

6 oz of cheddar cheese, crumbled

2 medium-sized carrots, sliced

2 medium-sized red onions, finely chopped

1 can of tomato sauce

1 garlic clove, crushed

1 medium-sized bell pepper, chopped

1 medium-sized zucchini, sliced

1 can of cherry tomatoes, halved

1 can of black beans, rinsed and drained

8 oz of frozen corn, thawed

1 tbsp of olive oil

1 tsp of dried oregano, ground

½ tsp of chili pepper, ground

¼ tsp of black pepper, ground

Preparation:

Preheat the oven to 375°F.

Preheat the oil in a large skillet over a medium-high temperature. Add garlic and onions, and stir-fry for 2-3 minutes. Now, add pepper, zucchini, and carrots and stir one again. Cook for another 10 minutes stirring constantly. Pour over the tomato sauce and canned tomatoes. Sprinkle with oregano and stir all well.

Cook until boils and reduce the heat to low. Cook for another 15 minutes stirring occasionally. Add beans and corn. Sprinkle with chili pepper and stir again. Cook for 5 minutes more and remove from the heat.

Gently stir in the pasta and cheeses. Transfer to a casserole dish. Put it in the oven and bake for 30 minutes. Remove from the oven and set aside for 5 minutes to cool. Serve warm.

Nutrition information per serving: Kcal: 440, Protein: 20.4g, Carbs: 59.3g, Fats: 17.1g

5. Avocado and Beet Salad

Ingredients:

1 medium-sized avocado, peeled and chopped

4 medium-sized beets, peeled and chopped

2 cups of cherry tomatoes, halved

1 medium-sized pear, cored and chopped

1 large carrot, sliced

2 tbsp of cashews, chopped

1 tbsp of olive oil

1 tbsp of balsamic vinegar

¼ tsp of Cayenne pepper, ground

¼ tsp of sea salt

¼ tsp of black pepper, ground

Preparation:

Place the beets in a large pot. Pour enough water to cover

all and bring it to a boil. Cook for 15 minutes or until fork-tender. Remove from the heat and drain. Set aside.

Combine vinegar, oil and cayenne pepper in a small mixing bowl. Whisk well and set aside.

Meanwhile, combine avocado chops, carrot, and cherry tomatoes in a large salad bowl. Add cooked beets and pour over the sauce. Stir all well and sprinkle with cashews, salt and pepper.

Serve immediately.

Nutrition information per serving: Kcal: 202, Protein: 2.7g, Carbs: 16.7g, Fats: 15.5g

6. Rice with Pears

Ingredients:

4 cups of brown rice, pre-cooked

2 large pears, cored and cubed

½ cup of spring onions, finely chopped

½ cup of fresh celery, diced

3 tbsp of vegetable oil

3 tbsp of lemon juice

2 garlic cloves, crushed

¼ tsp of black pepper, ground

¼ tsp of fresh ginger, ground

¼ tsp of salt

Preparation:

Combine garlic, ginger, salt, pepper, and lemon juice in a medium-sized bowl. Stir well and add pear cubes. Coat well and mix. Set aside.

Meanwhile, place rice in a large pot. Pour enough water to cover and bring it to a boil. Add spring onions, celery, and oil. Stir well and cook for until set. Remove from the heat and let it cool. Transfer to a serving bowl and gently stir in the pears mixture. Refrigerate for 20 minutes before serving.

Nutrition information per serving: Kcal: 527, Protein: 9.8g, Carbs: 98.1g, Fats: 10.3g

7. Salmon with Spinach in Dijon Sauce

Ingredients:

1 lb of salmon fillets, skinless and boneless

4 tbsp of Dijon mustard

1 tbsp of olive oil

1 tbsp of honey

1 tsp of dried dill

¼ tsp of salt

¼ tsp of black pepper, freshly ground

1 cup of spinach, chopped

2 garlic clove, minced

Preparation:

Combine honey, dill, mustard, salt, and pepper in a small bowl. Stir well to combine. Place filets in a large bowl and pour over the marinade. Coat the meat with a spoon and set aside for 1 hour.

Place spinach in a pot of boiling water. Cook for 5 minutes and remove from the heat. Drain and set aside.

Preheat the oil in a large frying pan over a medium-high temperature. Add garlic and stir-fry until translucent. Add the meat and reserve the marinade. Cook for about 3-5 minutes on both sides, or until flakes. Transfer the meat to a serving plate, but reserve the pan and reduce the heat to low. Add spinach cook for 10 minutes, stirring constantly. Remove from the heat and add it to the serving plate.

Drizzle with previously used marinade and sprinkle with some extra salt and pepper.

Nutrition information per serving: Kcal: 234, Protein: 23.4g, Carbs: 10.4g, Fats: 13.8g

8. Blackberry Mango Smoothie

Ingredients:

¼ cup of blackberries

1 small mango, cubed

1 large pear, chopped

3 tbsp of walnuts, roughly chopped

1 tbsp of honey

1 tsp of hempseed

1 cup of water

Preparation:

Combine all ingredients in a food processor. Blend until nicely smooth. Transfer to a serving glasses. Garnish with mint leaves and walnuts. Refrigerate for 1 hour before serving.

Nutrition information per serving: Kcal: 253, Protein: 4.8g, Carbs: 47.1g, Fats: 7.7g

9. Cucumber Salad with Tomato Vinaigrette

Ingredients:

2 large cucumbers

2 cups of Iceberg lettuce, chopped

1 small onion, sliced

1 tbsp of sour cream

3 tbsp of white wine vinegar

1 tsp of Worcestershire sauce

½ cup of sun-dried tomatoes, finely chopped

1 garlic clove, minced

1 tsp of parsley, finely chopped

1 tsp of honey

¼ tsp of black pepper, ground

2 tbsp of extra-virgin olive oil

Preparation:

Combine sour cream, Worcestershire sauce, vinegar, sun-dried tomatoes, garlic, honey, oil, pepper, and salt in a jar or a small mixing bowl. Stir well and seal with a lid. Refrigerate overnight to allow flavors to meld.

Combine cucumbers, lettuce, and onions in large salad bowl. Drizzle with marinade and sprinkle with fresh parsley.

Nutrition information per serving: Kcal: 179, Protein: 1.4g, Carbs: 11.2g, Fats: 15.4g

10. Cauliflower and Broccoli Soup

Ingredients:

1 lb of cauliflower, chopped

1 lb of broccoli, halved

5 cups of chicken broth

2 tbsp of olive oil

2 garlic cloves, minced

1 tbsp of Dijon mustard

1 tsp of vegetable seasoning mix

½ tsp of salt

Preparation:

Preheat the oil in a large pot over a medium-high temperature. Add garlic and stir-fry until translucent. Add cauliflower, broccoli, and salt. Pour over the stock and bring it all to a boil. Reduce the heat to low and simmer for 20 minutes, or until fork-tender. Remove from the heat and let it cool for a while.

Transfer to a food processor and blend for 2 minutes, or until nicely smooth. Add mustard and sprinkle with vegetable seasoning mix and re-blend.

Transfer the soup to a pot and cover. Add more chicken broth or water if it is too thick and heat it up again.

Serve warm.

Nutrition information per serving: Kcal: 120, Protein: 7.8g, Carbs: 10.3g, Fats: 6.2g

11. Chicken in Lemon & Rosemary Sauce

Ingredients:

1 chicken, (3-4 lb), whole

3 small potatoes, peeled and wedged

1 cup of lemon juice

1 tsp of dried rosemary

½ tsp of vegetable seasoning mix

¼ tsp of black pepper, ground

¼ tsp of salt

Preparation:

Preheat the grill over a medium-low temperature.

Combine lemon juice, rosemary, vegetable seasoning mix, pepper, and salt in a large baking dish. Stir well to combine. Cut the chicken in half in a put it in the bowl. Coat well the chicken with marinade. Cover and set aside to marinate for 2 hours.

Meanwhile, place potatoes in a pot of boiling water. Cook until fork-tender. Remove from the heat and let it cool. Cut into wedges and transfer to a baking dish with the meat.

Grill the chicken for 1 hour, turning several times until nicely golden brown. Remove from grill.

Garnish with fresh rosemary and serve.

Nutrition information per serving: Kcal: 309, Protein: 50.6g, Carbs: 10.8g, Fats: 5.5g

12. Leek Salad with Walnuts

Ingredients:

8 small leeks, chopped

2 garlic cloves, minced

¼ cup of shallots, minced

¼ cup of walnuts, roughly chopped

1 tsp of yellow mustard

2 tbsp of balsamic vinegar

2 tbsp of olive oil

1 tbsp of chives, minced

1 tsp of fresh parsley, finely chopped

¼ tsp of salt

¼ tsp of black pepper, ground

Preparation:

Combine garlic, shallots, mustard, and walnuts in a small

mixing bowl or a jar. Pour the vinegar and oil. Give it a good stir, or if using a jar, seal the lid. Sprinkle with parsley, chives, salt and pepper. Set aside for 30 minutes to allow flavors to mingle.

Meanwhile, place the leeks in a large saucepan over a medium-high temperature. Pour enough water to cover and bring it to a boil. Reduce the heat to low and cover with a lid. Simmer for about 10-12 minutes more, or until set. Remove from the heat and drain well. Transfer to a salad bowl.

Pour over the marinade over the leeks. Let it cool and refrigerate 10 minutes before serving.

Nutrition information per serving: Kcal: 121, Protein: 2.3g, Carbs: 3.2g, Fats: 11.7g

13. Fish Nuggets with Tomato Sauce

Ingredients:

8 oz of trout fillets, cubed

½ cup of breadcrumbs

1 large egg

2 tbsp of Greek yogurt

¼ cup of skim milk

1 tbsp of lemon juice

¼ tsp of salt

¼ tsp of black pepper, ground

For the sauce:

2 large tomatoes, pureed

1 tbsp of lemon juice

¼ tsp of chili pepper, ground

¼ tsp of dried oregano, ground

Preparation:

Preheat the oven to 375°F.

Combine tomatoes, chili, oregano and lemon juice in a food processor. Blend until smooth. Set aside.

Beat the egg in a medium-sized bowl. Add yogurt and milk. Sprinkle with some salt and pepper to taste and whisk well to combine.

Now, dip the fish into the egg mixture, then roll in breadcrumbs.

Place some baking paper on a baking sheet. Spread the fish evenly and put it in the oven. Bake until golden brown. Remove from the oven.

Serve baked nuggets with tomato sauce or simply drizzle over.

Nutrition information per serving: Kcal: 204, Protein: 19.8g, Carbs: 14.4g, Fats: 7.1g

14. Mint Strawberry Salad

Ingredients:

2 cups of strawberries, sliced

1 cup of arugula, chopped

½ cup of red cabbage, shredded

½ cup of dates, pitted and chopped

1 cup of Romaine lettuce, chopped

½ cup of sour cream

1 tbsp of fresh mint, ground

2 tbsp of orange juice

¼ tsp of salt

3-4 mint leaves

Preparation:

Combine sour cream, orange juice, ground mint, salt and pepper in a small mixing bowl. Stir well to combine and set aside to allow flavors to mingle.

Combine strawberries, arugula, cabbage, and dates in a large bowl. Stir once, then pour over the previously made sauce.

Garnish with mint leaves and refrigerate for 15 minutes before serving.

Nutrition information per serving: Kcal: 157, Protein: 2.3g, Carbs: 25.5g, Fats: 6.4g

15. Creamy Broccoli

Ingredients:

1 lb of broccoli, chopped

4 oz of cheddar cheese, shredded

3 tsp of cornstarch

1 cup of skim milk

1 tsp of Worcestershire sauce

¼ tsp black pepper, ground

½ tsp of salt

Preparation:

Place the broccoli in a pot of boiling water. Cook until fork-tender and remove from the heat. Drain well and set aside.

Combine cornstarch and milk in a large saucepan over a medium-high temperature. Bring it to a boil and reduce the heat to low. Cook until slightly thickened. Add cheese and sauce. Cook until cheese is melted. Remove from the heat and let it cool for a while.

Transfer broccoli portions into a serving plate. Pour over the sauce and serve.

Nutrition information per serving: Kcal: 185, Protein: 12.3g, Carbs: 13.1g, Fats: 9.8g

16. Turkey Wraps

Ingredients:

12 oz of turkey filets, minced

10 oz of tomatoes, finely chopped

1 small onion, sliced

3 garlic cloves, minced

3 tbsp of tomato sauce

1 tbsp of Worcestershire sauce

1 tsp of paprika, ground

1 tbsp of olive oil

½ tsp of salt

4 lettuce leaves

4 tortillas

Preparation:

Preheat the oil in large pot over a medium-high

temperature. Add onion and garlic and stir-fry until translucent. Add meat, tomatoes, tomato sauce and Worcestershire sauce. Sprinkle with a pinch of salt and stir well. Reduce the heat to low, cover with a lid and cook for 3 hours, or until set. Stir in the paprika and remove from the heat. Let it cool for a while.

Spread one lettuce leaf over the tortilla and spoon the mixture evenly. Wrap and secure with a toothpick.

Nutrition information per serving: Kcal: 259, Protein: 27.5g, Carbs: 17.7g, Fats: 8.7g

17. Spanish Style Chicken

Ingredients:

1 lb of chicken filets, skinless and boneless, chopped

1 cup of chicken broth

2 tbsp of all-purpose flour

2 bell peppers, cut into strips

1 large onion, wedged

2 medium-sized tomatoes, diced

2 tbsp of olive oil

2 garlic cloves, crushed

¼ tsp of Cayenne pepper, ground

¼ tsp of salt

¼ tsp of black pepper, ground

Preparation:

Combine meat chops, flour and salt in a large bowl. Toss

well to combine and set aside.

Preheat the oil in a large nonstick skillet over a medium-high temperature. Add garlic and stir-fry until translucent. Add meat and cook until golden brown. Reduce the heat to low and add tomatoes, peppers, and onion wedges. Sprinkle with cayenne pepper and salt to taste.

Pour over the chicken broth and let it simmer for 15 minutes. Sprinkle with extra salt and pepper to taste.

Nutrition information per serving: Kcal: 303, Protein: 36.1g, Carbs: 14.2g, Fats: 11.2g

18. Creamy Fennel Soup

Ingredients:

1 medium-sized fennel bulb, chopped

2 cups of vegetable broth

1 cup of skim milk

1 cup of white quinoa, pre-cooked

2 garlic cloves, minced

½ tsp of salt

¼ tsp of black pepper, ground

Preparation:

Combine fennel, milk, quinoa, garlic and vegetable broth in a deep pot over a medium-high temperature. Bring it to a boil and then reduce the heat to low. Cover with a lid and cook for about 10-15 minutes more. Remove from the heat and let it cool for a while.

Transfer the soup to a food processor and blend until nicely smooth. Return the soup to the pot. Reheat the soup and serve warm.

Nutrition information per serving: Kcal: 146, Protein: 7.5g, Carbs: 23.7g, Fats: 2.3g

19. Bean Risotto

Ingredients:

2 cups of white rice, pre-cooked

1 cup of frozen beans, thawed

1 cup of button mushrooms, halved

2 cups of vegetable broth

1 small onion, finely chopped

1 tsp of balsamic vinegar

2 tbsp of olive oil

½ tsp of salt

¼ tsp of black pepper, ground

2 cups of water

Preparation:

Combine vegetable broth and water in a deep pot and bring it to a boil. Add rice, beans, and mushrooms. Reduce the heat to low and cover with a lid.

Meanwhile, preheat the oil in a large saucepan and add onion. Stir-fry until translucent. Add vinegar and saute for 1 minute. Remove from the heat and transfer to the pot.

Cook water until water evaporates, or until set. Add more water if needed.

Serve warm.

Nutrition information per serving: Kcal: 291, Protein: 6.5g, Carbs: 52.2g, Fats: 5.6g

20. Pumpkin Oatmeal with Pecans

Ingredients:

2 cups of oats

2 cups of pumpkin, peeled, pre-cooked, and chopped

3 cups of skim milk

¼ tsp of cinnamon

¼ cup of pecans, roughly chopped

¼ cup of prunes, chopped

Preparation:

Prepare oats using package instructions, or combine it with milk and microwave it for 2-3 minutes.

Place pumpkin chops in a pot of boiling water and cook until tender. Remove from the heat and drain well. Cut into bite-sized pieces and stir into prepared oats with milk. Sprinkle with cinnamon and reheat for 1 minute. Stir in the pecans and prunes before serving.

Nutrition information per serving: Kcal: 387, Protein: 17.3g, Carbs: 71.3g, Fats: 4.1g

21. Baked Mozzarella Eggplants

Ingredients:

1 large eggplant, peeled and cut into bite-sized pieces

6 oz of mozzarella cheese, thinly sliced

3 large tomatoes, chopped

¼ tsp of dried rosemary, ground

¼ tsp of salt

¼ chili pepper, ground

¼ tsp of black pepper, ground

Preparation:

Preheat the oven to 375°F.

Combine tomatoes, rosemary, salt, chili, and pepper in a blender. Blend until smooth and set aside.

Place some baking paper on a large baking dish. Make one layer of mozzarella slices, and top with eggplant chops. Make another layer of cheese and pour over the tomato sauce to coat all well. Sprinkle with some extra salt and pepper to taste. Put it in the oven and bake for 30 minutes. remove from the oven and let it cool for a while.

Serve warm.

Nutrition information per serving: Kcal: 116, Protein: 9.6g, Carbs: 9.1g, Fats: 5.3g

22. Creamy Cranberry Salad

Ingredients:

1 cup of fresh cranberries, chopped

½ medium-sized pineapple, chopped

1 medium-sized green apple, chopped

1 tbsp of honey

2 cups of whipped cream

1 tbsp of almonds, roughly chopped

1tbsp of chia seeds

Preparation:

Combine whipped cream, almonds, and honey in a large bowl. Mix well, using a hand mixer. Set aside.

Combine cranberries, pineapple, and apple in a large bowl. Pour over the previously made cream. Sprinkle with chia seeds and refrigerate 30 minutes before serving.

Nutrition information per serving: Kcal: 254, Protein: 5.8g, Carbs: 18.6g, Fats: 20.4g

23. Marinated Tuna with Spinach

Ingredients:

1 lb of tuna steaks, boneless

2 cups of spinach, chopped

1 small red onion, sliced

2 tbsp of olive oil

1 tbsp of lime juice

1 tbsp of lemon juice

2 tsp of cilantro, finely chopped

2 tsp of cumin, ground

1 tsp of sea salt

½ tsp of black pepper, ground

Preparation:

Place the spinach in a pot of boiling water and cook until soften. Remove from the heat and drain well. Set aside.

Combine lime juice, lemon juice, cilantro, cumin, salt, and pepper to a large marinade bowl. Place the meat and coat well. Cover and set aside to marinate for 20 minutes. Turn the meat occasionally and coat with a spoon.

Preheat the grill to a medium-high temperature. Grill the meat for about 2-3 minutes on each side or until set.

Serve with spinach and top with onion slices.

Nutrition information per serving: Kcal: 285, Protein: 34.8g, Carbs: 3.1g, Fats: 14.5g

24. Grape Cheese Salad

Ingredients:

1 lb of red grapes

1 lb of green grapes

8 oz of cream cheese, softened

1 tbsp of honey

1 tsp of vanilla extract

3 tbsp of pecans, roughly chopped

Preparation:

Combine cream cheese, vanilla extract, and honey in large bowl. Beat well until nicely smooth. Add grapes and stir all well to combine. Cover and refrigerate 30 minutes. Top with pecans before serving.

Nutrition information per serving: Kcal: 295, Protein: 4.6g, Carbs: 35.9g, Fats: 16.5g

25. Coconut Shrimps

Ingredients:

12 oz of shrimps, peeled and deveined

½ cup of coconut milk

4 garlic cloves, minced

1 tbsp of olive oil

1 tbsp of fresh coriander, finely chopped

1 tsp of lemon juice

¼ tsp of salt

Preparation:

Place the rice in a large pot. Pour enough water to cover all ingredients. Cook until water evaporates, or until set. Remove from the heat and set aside.

Preheat the oil in a deep pot or a slow cooker over a medium-high temperature. Add garlic and stir-fry until translucent. Add shrimps and cook for about 2-3 minutes more.

Add all other ingredients and stir once. Seal the lid and cook for at least 5 hours. Remove from the heat and let it stay for a while before you open the lid.

Serve with rice.

Nutrition information per serving: Kcal: 410, Protein: 40.5g, Carbs: 7.9g, Fats: 24.2g

26. Red Peperonata

Ingredients:

2 tbsp of olive oil

1 small onion, sliced

2 garlic clove, chopped

1 red capsicum pepper, chopped

2 small tomatoes, sliced

1 tbsp of apple vinegar

2 tbsp of olive oil

4-5 fresh basil leaves

¼ tsp of salt

¼ tsp of black pepper, ground

Preparation:

Heat up the olive oil in a large saucepan over medium temperature. Add sliced onion and stir-fry for few minutes, until golden color. Add garlic and capsicum pepper. Season with salt and pepper. Fry for 15 minutes, stirring constantly.

Reduce the heat to low and add tomatoes. Cover and cook for few minutes. Remove from the heat and serve.

Nutrition information per serving: Kcal: 296, Protein: 2.1g, Carbs: 12.1g, Fats: 28.3g

27. Sweet Apricot Risotto

Ingredients:

1 cup of brown rice, pre-cooked

¼ cup of dried apricots, chopped

1 large cucumber, peeled and sliced

2 medium-sized carrots, grated

1 small tomato, diced

1 medium-sized red onion, sliced

2 tbsp of olive oil

1 tsp of vegetable seasoning mix

1 tbsp of fresh parsley, finely chopped

¼ tsp of salt

Preparation:

Place the rice in a deep pot. Pour 2 ½ cups of water and bring it to a boil. Remove from the heat and set aside.

Preheat the oil in a large frying skillet over a medium-high temperature. Add onions and saute until soften. Stir in the diced tomato, apricots and sprinkle with vegetable seasoning mix. Cook for about 4-5 minutes. Stir in the rice, cook for 1 minute and remove from the heat.

Transfer to a serving plate and top with grated carrots. Garnish with fresh cucumber slices and sprinkle with fresh parsley.

Serve.

Nutrition information per serving: Kcal: 221, Protein: 4.1g, Carbs: 37.2g, Fats: 6.8g

28. Cabbage and Tomato Salad with Rice Vinegar Dressing

Ingredients:

1 small cabbage head, sliced

2 medium-sized tomatoes, cubed

1 cup of radicchio, grated

1 medium-sized bell pepper, cubed

For the dressing:

2 tbsp of rice vinegar

2 tbsp of fresh cilantro, finely chopped

2 tbsp of extra-virgin olive oil

¼ tsp of black pepper, ground

¼ tsp of sea salt

Preparation:

Combine all dressing ingredients in a mixing bowl. Stir well and set aside to allow flavors to mingle.

In a large salad bowl, combine cabbage, tomatoes, radicchio, and pepper. Toss and drizzle with dressing. Give it a good stir and refrigerate 20 minutes before serving. You can stir in 2 tablespoons of sour cream if you like, but this is, however, optional.

Nutrition information per serving: Kcal: 144, Protein: 3.3g, Carbs: 15.5g, Fats: 7.4g

29. Oven-Baked Sea Bass

Ingredients:

2 lb of Sea bass fillets, boneless

¼ cup of skim milk

2 tbsp of lemon juice

½ cup of breadcrumbs

1 garlic clove, minced

1 small onion, sliced

1 medium-sized lemon, wedged

¼ tsp of white pepper, ground

¼ tsp of chili pepper, ground

½ tsp of sea salt

1 tbsp of fresh rosemary, finely chopped

Preparation:

Preheat the oven to 375°F.

Combine milk, crushed garlic, and chili pepper in medium bowl. Set aside.

Wash and pat dry the fish. Place it in a bowl and coat well with lemon juice. Transfer the fish to a bowl with milk. Let it stay for 15 minutes to let fish soak the liquid.

Spread the breadcrumbs over a clean baking sheet. Coat the filets in breadcrumbs.

Grease a large baking sheet with oil and place the filets into it. Put it in the oven and bake for about 20-25 minutes. Remove from the heat and serve with lemon wedges.

Nutrition information per serving: Kcal: 236, Protein: 37.5g, Carbs: 8.8g, Fats: 4.5g

30. Apple Kale Smoothie

Ingredients:

1 large apple, cored and chopped

1 cup of kale, chopped

½ cup of skim milk

1 tbsp of honey

1 tbsp of flaxseeds

Preparation:

Place kale in a pot of boiling water. Cook until soften and remove from the heat. Drain well and set aside to cool for a while.

Now, combine cooked kale and all other ingredients in a food processor. Blend until nicely smooth. Transfer to a serving glasses and refrigerate for 1 hour before serving.

Nutrition information per serving: Kcal: 147, Protein: 4.1g, Carbs: 31.2g, Fats: 1.3g

31. Turkey with Kiwi Pasta

Ingredients:

1 lb of turkey breasts, chopped

8 oz of pasta (noodles)

2 cups of broccoli, halved

4 large kiwis, peeled and sliced

2 medium-sized bell peppers, cut into strips

½ cup of spring onions, chopped

4 tbsp of Parmesan cheese, grated

½ tsp of salt

For the dressing:

2 tbsp of olive oil

½ cup of balsamic vinegar

2 tbsp of yellow mustard

2 tsp of fresh basil, finely chopped

Preparation:

Place meat in a large saucepan and pour enough water to cover it. Sprinkle with salt to taste. Cover with a lid and cook for 1 hour over a medium-low temperature. Remove from the heat and drain. Set aside.

Combine dressing ingredients in a mixing bowl. Whisk well and set aside to allow flavors to meld.

Use package instructions to cook noodles. Just before the set, add broccoli stir well. Cook for about 1-2 minutes more and remove from the heat. Drain well and drizzle with previously made dressing.

Stir in the kiwis, peppers, spring onions and toss well to combine. Top with cooked meat chops and sprinkle with cheese. Serve.

Nutrition information per serving: Kcal: 217, Protein: 14.4g, Carbs: 27.6g, Fats: 5.6g

32. Apple Quinoa Smoothie

Ingredients:

1 large green apple, cored and chopped

1 cup of white quinoa, pre-cooked

1 cup of baby spinach, chopped and pre-cooked

½ medium-sized cucumber, sliced

1 cup of water

Preparation:

Place quinoa in a medium pot and pour enough water to cover it. Cook until set and remove from the heat. Drain and transfer to a medium bowl.

Use the same pot and repeat the process for spinach. Drain and combine with quinoa. Add all other ingredients and transfer all to a food processor. Blend until nicely smooth. Refrigerate for 30 minutes and top with mint leaves before serving.

Nutrition information per serving: Kcal: 110, Protein: 4.2g, Carbs: 22.1g, Fats: 1.5g

33. Salmon with Basil sauce

Ingredients:

5 oz of salmon filets, skinless and boneless

12 oz of baby carrots, whole

12 oz of broccoli, chopped

2 tbsp of fresh basil, finely chopped

8 garlic cloves, minced

½ cup of olive oil

1 medium-sized lemon, wedged

1 tsp of salt

Preparation:

Combine carrots and broccoli in a large pot. Pour water enough to cover all ingredients. Cook until fork-tender. Remove from the heat and drain well. Sprinkle with a pinch of salt and set aside.

Combine garlic and salt in a food processor and blend.

Gradually add about 1 teaspoon at a time. Blend 30 seconds in between. Repeat the process until done. Add basil and pepper at the end and re-blend. Set aside.

Preheat one tablespoon of oil in a large baking sheet over a medium-high temperature. Broil for about 3-4 minutes on both sides, or until flakes. Remove from the oven and transfer to a serving plate. Pour over the garlic and basil sauce. Serve with cooked vegetables. Garnish with lemon wedges.

Nutrition information per serving: Kcal: 331, Protein: 10.2g, Carbs: 14.7g, Fats: 27.8g

34. Spinach Tomato Omelet

Ingredients:

8 large eggs

½ cup of spinach, chopped

1 large bell pepper, diced

2 small tomatoes, diced

1 small onion, diced

2 tbsp of olive oil

1 tbsp of skim milk

1 tsp of vegetable seasoning mix

¼ tsp of salt

¼ tsp of black pepper, ground

Preparation:

Place the spinach in a deep pot. Add 2 cups of water and bring it to a boil. Remove from the heat and drain well. Set aside to cool.

Combine tomatoes and milk in a blender. Add a pinch of salt and blend until nicely smooth. Set aside.

Preheat the oil in a nonstick skillet over a medium-high temperature. Add onion and stir-fry until translucent. Add chopped pepper and cook for about 4-5 minutes more. Add spinach and pour over the tomato sauce.

Whisk the eggs in a mixing bowl and add a pinch of salt, pepper, and vegetable seasoning mix. Cook until eggs are done. Fold the omelet using a spatula and remove from the heat.

Serve immediately.

Nutrition information per serving: Kcal: 230, Protein: 13.7g, Carbs: 6.8g, Fats: 17.1g

35. Mackerel Salad

Ingredients:

3 mackerel fillets, boneless

1 tbsp of olive oil

1 tsp of dried rosemary, ground

1 cup of cherry tomatoes

¼ cup of olives

1 tsp of garlic, minced

1 tsp of dried basil, ground

2 tbsp of lemon juice

¼ tsp of salt

Preparation:

Sprinkle the mackerel fillets with rosemary and fry in a large saucepan at 350 degrees for about 10 minutes on each side, or until nice golden color. Use a kitchen paper to soak the excess oil. Allow it to cool for about 15 minutes and cut into equal cubes.

Mix the fish with other ingredients in a large bowl. Add garlic, basil and lemon juice. Salt to taste and serve warm.

Nutrition information per serving: Kcal: 299, Protein: 21.8g, Carbs: 3.8g, Fats: 21.8g

36. Zucchini Salmon

Ingredients:

1 lb of salmon fillets, sliced

2 small zucchinis

6 Brussels sprouts

3 tbsp of extra-virgin olive oil

¼ tsp of black pepper, ground

Preparation:

Peel and slice zucchinis into 0.5-inch thick circle shape slices. Cut salmon fillets into bite size pieces. Heat up one tbsp of olive oil in a large skillet and add your salmon fillets. Fry them up for about 10 minutes, or until they are nice and crispy. When done, move them to a plate covered with a kitchen paper to soak up the grease. Set aside.

Cut the Brussels sprouts in half. Combine with zucchini slices in a large bowl and add 2 tbsp of the remaining olive oil. Move the vegetables to the skillet and cook until the Brussel sprouts are tender. It should take no more than 10 minutes. Add your salmon fillets to the skillet, cover and allow it to rewarm. Serve and enjoy.

Nutrition information per serving: Kcal: 262, Protein: 23.7g, Carbs: 4.7g, Fats: 17.7g

37. Shrimps in Tomato Sauce

Ingredients:

3 cups of frozen shrimps, thawed

3 medium-sized tomatoes, roughly chopped

1 tsp of dried basil, ground

3 garlic cloves, chopped

¼ tsp of black pepper, ground

¼ cup of olive oil

3 tbsp of olive oil (for frying)

Preparation:

Whisk together ¼ cup of olive oil, dried basil, chopped garlic, and pepper in a mixing bowl. Brush each shrimp with this marinade and set aside. Wash and roughly chop the tomatoes.

Use a large grill pan to heat up 3 tbsp of olive oil. Remove the shrimps from the marinade and grill for few minutes on each side. You want to get a lightly golden brown color.

Reduce the heat to minimum and add chopped tomatoes. Cover and cook until tomatoes soften. Serve warm.

Nutrition information per serving: Kcal: 218, Protein: 1.1g, Carbs: 4.4g, Fats: 23.3g

38. Spicy Apple Puree

Ingredients:

1 cup of homemade apple puree

½ cup of olive oil

4 tbsp of apple cider vinegar

3 tbsp of dried parsley, chopped

2 tbsp of dried marjoram, ground

¼ tsp of red pepper, ground

¼ tbsp of yellow mustard

For homemade apple puree:

5-6 medium sized apples (Alkmene apple)

1 tsp of cinnamon, ground

4 cups of water

Preparation:

Wash and peel the apples. Cut into quarters and remove

the core. Place them in a large pot and pour enough water to cover them (4 cups will do the job). Bring them to a boiling point and keep cooking until soft. Stir occasionally. After about 20 minutes, remove from the heat and drain. Allow it to cool for a while and mash with a fork. Place in a food processor with one tsp of ground cinnamon. Mix for 30 seconds, or until smooth mixture. Pour in a tall jar and cover with a tight lid.

Useful tip: Prepare the apple puree several hours earlier, perhaps even a day earlier. For this recipe, you want a nice and cold apple pure.

Now you want to prepare your starter. Whisk olive oil, apple vinegar, ground red pepper and mustard in a large bowl. You need a smooth mixture. Combine it with an apple puree and add dried parsley and dried marjoram. Let it stand in the refrigerator for about an hour. You can serve your healthy starter.

Nutrition information per serving: Kcal: 298, Protein: 0.9g, Carbs: 32.3g, Fats: 20.7g

39.   Turkey Cacciatore

Ingredients:

4 chicken breasts, skinless and boneless

12 oz of sun-dried tomato paste

2 small onions, sliced

1 cup of chicken broth, unsalted

2 garlic cloves, crushed

1 tsp of dried basil, ground

½ tsp of dried oregano, ground

¼ tsp of black pepper, ground

¼ tsp of salt

1 cup of water

Preparation:

Combine all ingredients in a slow cooker. Seal the lid and cook for about 9-10 hours on a low temperature. Remove from the heat and let it stand for a while before you open it.

Sprinkle with extra salt, pepper or chili to taste. Serve warm.

Nutrition information per serving: Kcal: 242, Protein: 30.6g, Carbs: 13.5g, Fats: 7.5g

40. Cheese Watermelon Salad

Ingredients:

4 cups of watermelon, seeded and chopped

½ cup of Feta cheese, crumbled

¼ cup of olives, pitted and finely chopped

1 tbsp of fresh basil, finely chopped

1 small red onion, sliced

2 tbsp of extra-virgin olive oil

3 tbsp of lemon juice

Preparation:

Combine lemon juice, olive oil, basil, and salt in a mixing bowl. Mix well to combine and set aside for 10 minutes to allow flavors to meld.

Combine watermelon, onion, basil and olives in large salad bowl. Drizzle with marinade and toss well. Refrigerate for 30 minutes before serving.

Nutrition information per serving: Kcal: 175, Protein: 3.8g, Carbs: 14.6g, Fats: 12.2g

41. Creamy Roasted Veggies

Ingredients:

½ cup of beetroot, peeled and diced

½ cup of Brussel sprouts, chopped

½ cup of pumpkin, peeled and chopped

½ cup of carrot, chopped

1 cup of tomatoes, roughly chopped

½ cup of roasted tomatoes

1 small onion, sliced

2 garlic cloves, minced

1 cup of silverbeet, finely chopped

½ tsp of salt

¼ tsp of black pepper, ground

3 tbsp of olive oil

Preparation:

Preheat the oven to 350°F.

In a large bowl, combine beetroot, Brussels sprouts and pumpkin. Add 1 tbsp of olive oil and some salt to taste. Place on an oven tray and bake for about 20 minutes.

Meanwhile, heat up the remaining oil in a medium sized saucepan. Add onions and carrot and fry for about 5 minutes, stirring constantly.

Add diced tomatoes and silverbeet. Season with pepper and gently simmer for about 20 minutes. Stir once and then add silverbeet, salt, and pepper.

Serve warm.

Nutrition information per serving: Kcal: 138, Protein: 1.9g, Carbs: 10.9g, Fats: 10.8g

42. Pumpkin Starter

Ingredients:

2 cups of pumpkin, chopped

2 tsp of fresh cumin, ground

2 tsp of coriander, ground

4 tbsp of vegetable oil

8 dried figs, sliced

1 small red onion, sliced

¼ cup of fresh coriander, chopped

4 tbsp of fresh lemon juice

¼ cup of olive oil

Preparation:

Preheat the oven to 300°F.

In a large bowl, combine the pumpkin with cumin, coriander, and vegetable. Mix well. Spread this pumpkin mixture on a baking sheet and bake for about 20 minutes.

Remove from the oven and allow it to cool.

Place pumpkin, figs, onion, coriander leaves, lemon rind, lemon juice and olive oil into a bowl and toss gently to coat. Serve.

Nutrition information per serving: Kcal: 379, Protein: 3.1g, Carbs: 36.6g, Fats: 27.3g

43. Cherry Pancakes

Ingredients:

1 cup of all-purpose flour

2 large eggs

4 tsp of sugar

1 tsp of vanilla extract

1 tsp of baking powder

1 cup of skim milk

1 cup of fresh cherries

3 tsp of cherry extract

¼ cup of fresh cherry juice

2 tbsp of oil (for frying)

Preparation:

Combine all dry ingredients in a large bowl. Mix well and gently whisk in 1 cup of milk, vanilla extract, and eggs. Cover and let it stand for about 10 minutes.

Meanwhile, preheat the oil in a medium nonstick frying pan over a medium-sized temperature. About 1 tablespoon of oil will be enough for the first two pancakes. You can add some more oil later.

Pour some pancake mixture onto the frying pan. Fry for about a minute on each side, or until light brown color on both sides. Transfer to a plate.

In another bowl, combine 2 cups of fresh cherries with cherry extract. Whisk in ¼ cup of fresh cherry juice. Top each pancake with 2 tablespoons of this mixture and serve.

Nutrition information per serving: Kcal: 251, Protein: 8.4g, Carbs: 31.4g, Fats: 9.6g

44.   Italian Shrimps

Ingredients:

1 lb of large shrimps, peeled and deveined

2 tbsp of lemon juice

2 lemons, cut into thin slices

5 tbsp of olive oil

½ tsp of sea salt

½ tsp of red pepper, ground

½ tsp of black pepper, ground

1 tbsp of garlic, minced

10 bay leaves

Preparation:

Wash and drain your shrimps. In a large bowl combine lemon juice, 3 tablespoons of olive oil, sea salt, black and red pepper, bay leaves, and garlic to make a marinade. Soak the shrimps in it. Cover the bowl and leave in the refrigerator for about 10 minutes.

Heat up 2 tablespoons of olive oil at a high temperature in a grill saucepan. Fry shrimps for about 15 minutes, stirring constantly. If necessary, add some marinade while frying.

Nutrition information per serving: Kcal: 252, Protein: 21.6g, Carbs: 4.2g, Fats: 17.6g

45. Grilled Beef with Almonds

Ingredients:

3 large beef steaks

1 large onion, thinly sliced

4 cups of baby spinach, chopped

1 tsp of garlic, chopped

½ tsp of ginger, minced

¼ cup of lemon juice

¼ cup of almonds, roughly chopped

1 tbsp of lime juice

2 tbsp of water

1 tbsp of organic fish sauce, sugar-free

4 tbsp of vegetable oil

Preparation:

Wash and pat dry the beef steaks. Cut into bite size pieces

and set aside.

Peel the onion and cut into thin slices. Heat up the oil over a medium-high temperature and stir-fry the onions until golden brown.

Add chopped baby spinach and garlic. Mix well and fry for 5 minutes, until the water from the spinach evaporates. Stir well and remove from the heat.

In a large bowl combine the baby spinach with ginger, lemon juice, water, almonds and fish sauce. Mix well with a fork. Soak the beef steak pieces in it and return to saucepan. Add some more water if necessary. Cook over a low temperature for about 30 minutes, stirring occasionally.

When the water evaporates, remove from the heat and add lime juice. Allow it to cool for about 20-30 minutes and serve.

Nutrition information per serving: Kcal: 245, Protein: 3.9g, Carbs: 9.1g, Fats: 22.5g

46. Veal Kebab

Ingredients:

2 small sweet potatoes, peeled and cut into thin slices

2 veal steaks, cut into cubes

1 medium red onion, sliced

1 red pepper, sliced

3 tbsp fresh parsley, finely chopped

3 tbsp of fresh mint, finely chopped

3 tbsp of chives, finely chopped

2 small tomatoes, sliced

6 tbsp of olive oil

For the marinade:

2 tbsp of lemon juice

2 green chilies, seeded and finely chopped

2 small garlic cloves, finely chopped

4 tbsp of olive oil

2 tbsp white wine vinegar

Preparation:

Boil the potatoes for about 20-25 minutes, or until fork-tender. Drain and allow it to cool.

Combine lemon juice, green chilies, chopped garlic cloves, olive oil, and vinegar in a large mixing bowl. Soak the meat and the vegetables into this marinade and let it stand in the refrigerator for at least one hour.

Arrange the meat and vegetables on wooden sticks. Use a kitchen brush to spread the remaining olive oil over the kebabs. Grill directly over a medium-high temperature for about 5-6 minutes on each side.

Nutrition information per serving: Kcal: 375, Protein: 19.2g, Carbs: 11.1g, Fats: 28.4g

47. Peppermint Cookies

Ingredients:

1 cup of butter, softened

2 tbsp of honey

2 large eggs

1 tsp of peppermint extract

2 cups of all-purpose flour

½ cup of cocoa powder

1 tsp of baking soda

½ tsp of salt

1 cup of chocolate chips

Preparation:

Preheat the oven to 375°F.

Melt the butter and transfer it to a large mixing bowl. Add honey, eggs, peppermint extract. Whisk well until nicely smooth and fluffy. Set aside.

Combine flour, baking soda, salt, and cocoa powder. Stir well and add previously made butter mixture. Blend well using a hand mixer. Add chocolate chips and stir once again.

Make 1 inch thick balls using hands. Spread the balls on a large nonstick baking sheet. Press with the palm of your hand each cookie to form shape.

Put it in the oven and bake for 10 minutes or until crisp. Remove from the heat and let it cool for a while.

Serve or store in cookie jars up to 1 week.

Nutrition information per serving: Kcal: 153, Protein: 2.4g, Carbs: 14.1g, Fats: 10.1g

48. Kidney Bean Tuna Salad

Ingredients:

2 cups of white kidney beans, pre-cooked

1 can of tuna (Albacore), minced

1 cup of fresh celery, chopped

1 cup of bell peppers, chopped

¼ cup of spring onions, chopped

4 cups of Iceberg lettuce

1 cup of feta cheese

2 tbsp of olive oil

2 tbsp of balsamic vinegar

2 tbsp of Dijon mustard

1 tbsp of fresh basil, finely chopped

¼ tsp of black pepper, ground

½ tsp of salt

Preparation:

Place the beans in a pot of boiling water. Cook until soften. Remove from the heat and drain well. Set aside.

Combine mustard, basil, vinegar, oil, salt, and pepper in a mixing bowl. Set aside for 10 minutes to allow flavors to meld.

Combine tuna, beans, celery, pepper, and spring onions in a medium bowl. Stir all well to combine. Drizzle with marinade and give it a good stir.

Place a handful of lettuce on a serving plate and spoon the salad onto it. Top with cheese and serve.

Nutrition information per serving: Kcal: 386, Protein: 26.7g, Carbs: 41.6g, Fats: 13.3g

49. Green Chicken

Ingredients:

1 lb of chicken breasts, skinless and boneless

2 cups of spinach, chopped

1 cup of fresh orange juice

3 green bell peppers, chopped

3 small chili peppers, finely chopped

2 small onions, chopped

1 tbsp of fresh ginger, grated

1 tsp of red pepper powder, ground

4 tbsp of vegetable oil

½ tsp of salt

Preparation:

Wash and pat dry the chicken using a kitchen paper. Chop into bite size pieces. Finely chop the onions and peppers and set aside.

Heat up the oil in a large weasel over a medium-high temperature. Add onions and peppers and sauté until onions translucent. Now, add meat, ginger, red pepper powder, and salt. Cook for about 10-12 minutes, or until the chicken golden brown.

Meanwhile, combine fresh orange juice with spinach in a food processor. Mix well for 30 seconds. Add this mixture to the weasel and cook until the spinach gets well mashed. Cover the weasel, remove from the heat and let it stand for about 10 minutes before serving.

Nutrition information per serving: Kcal: 278, Protein: 23.4g, Carbs: 12.2g, Fats: 15.1g

50. Fish Stew

Ingredients:

1 lb of carp fillets

5 medium-sized carrots, sliced

3 chili peppers, sliced

3 medium-sized tomatoes, roughly chopped

¼ tsp of black pepper, ground

¼ cup of celery, finely chopped

1 tbsp of olive oil

Preparation:

Peel the carrots and wash thoroughly in cold water. Cut into thin slices. Cook carrots in a pot of boiling water for about 20 minutes, or until tender. Remove from the heat and drain. Set aside.

Heat up the olive oil in a large pot. Add carrots and fry for about 5 minutes, stirring constantly. Now, add sliced chili peppers, tomatoes, celery, and peppers. Fry the vegetables over a low temperature for about 8-10 minutes.

Meanwhile, wash and cut fillets into 1 inch-thick chops. Add fillets and 2 cups of water in a pot. Bring it to boil and cover. Reduce the heat to minimum and cook for about 30 minutes.

Nutrition information per serving: Kcal 378: , Protein: 28.6g, Carbs: 11.6g, Fats: 23.9g

51. Beef Chop with Pineapple & Turmeric

Ingredients:

1 ½ lb of beef chop, boneless

2 tbsp of coconut oil

1 tbsp of olive oil

½ cup of coconut milk

1 tsp of turmeric, ground

¼ tsp of black pepper, ground

1 medium-sized pineapple, peeled and chopped

Preparation:

Wash and dry the meat. Cut into bite size cubes. Combine the meat with coconut oil, coconut milk, turmeric, pepper, and pineapple. Mix well and set aside for 15 minutes.

Use a large wok pan to heat up the olive oil. Remove te meat and pineapple chops from the marinade and fry for about 5-7 minutes on each side. Now pour the remaining marinade, cover the wok pan and cook for 30 minutes over a medium temperature. The marinade will become thick and the meat soft. Remove from the heat and serve.

Nutrition information per serving: Kcal: 317, Protein: 34.9g, Carbs: 1.4g, Fats: 18.7g

52. Turkey Drumsticks with Nutmeg and Carob

Ingredients:

3 turkey legs

½ cup of almond milk

4 tsp of nutmeg, ground

3 tbsp of carob, minced

¼ tsp of red pepper, ground

Preparation:

Preheat the oven to 350°F.

Meanwhile, wash and clean the meat. Pat dry using a kitchen paper. In a small bowl, combine the almond milk, nutmeg, and carob. Mix well and soak each turkey leg with this mixture.

Sprinkle with red pepper to taste and wrap each turkey leg in aluminum foil.

Place the wrapped drumsticks on a baking sheet and cook for 40 minutes. Remove from the oven and allow to cool for a while before serving.

Nutrition information per serving: Kcal: 316, Protein: 31.2g, Carbs: 8.4g, Fats: 17.4g

53. Mustard Chicken

Ingredients:

2 chicken breasts, boneless and skinless

¼ cup of apple cider vinegar

¼ cup of olive oil

1 tbsp of garlic, minced

2 tbsp of yellow mustard

¼ tsp of green pepper, ground

1 tbsp of olive oil (for frying)

Preparation:

Wash and pat dry your meat. Place it on a cutting board and season with ground green pepper. In a large bowl, combine the apple vinegar, olive oil, garlic and mustard to make a marinade. Soak the chicken breast into this marinade and make sure it all gets coated nicely. Cover and place in the refrigerator for at least 2 hours (the best option is to keep it in the refrigerator overnight).

Preheat the oil in a large nonstick skillet over a medium-high temperature. Add chicken breasts and cook for about 7-10 minutes on each side, or until crispy and light brown. Add some of the marinade mixture while frying the chicken. These juices will make the meat soft.

Stir occasionally and cook until meat is set. Remove from the heat and serve.

Nutrition information per serving: Kcal 365: , Protein: 33.3g, Carbs: 1.3g, Fats: 24.8g

54. Eggplant Casserole

Ingredients:

2 large eggplants, peeled and sliced

1 cup of veal, minced

1 medium-sized onion, chopped

1 tsp of olive oil

2 medium-sized tomatoes, chopped

1 tsp of fresh parsley, finely chopped

¼ tsp of black pepper, ground

Preparation:

Preheat the oven to 300°F.

Peel the eggplants and cut lengthwise into thin sheets. Put them in a bowl, and leave them aside for at least an hour.

Roll eggplants in beaten eggs. Preheat the oil in a large skillet over a medium-high temperature. Place the eggplants slices and cook for 5 minutes on both sides, or until nicely soften. Remove from the pan and add onions. Now, add sliced peppers, tomato, and finely chopped parsley. Fry for few minutes and then add the meat.

When meat is tender, remove from heat, cool, add one egg and season with pepper. Put fried eggplant and meat with vegetables in the ovenproof dish and make layers until you have used all the material. Bake for 30 minutes, or until set.

Remove from the oven and let it cool for a while. Serve.

Nutrition information per serving: Kcal: 144, Protein: 9.6g, Carbs: 21.2g, Fats: 3.7g

55. Leek with Chicken Cubes

Ingredients:

2 cups of leeks, trimmed

1 cup of chicken fillets, cubed

3 tbsp of olive oil

1 tsp thyme leaves

¼ tsp of black pepper, ground

Preparation:

Cut the leeks into small pieces and wash it under cold water, a day before cooking. Leave it overnight in a plastic bag.

Preheat the oil in a large saucepan over a medium-high temperature. Add chicken cubes and cook for about 10-15 minutes. Stir constantly until the meat is nice and soft.

Reduce the temperature, add leeks, and mix well. Cook for about 5-7 more minutes. When done, remove from the saucepan and sprinkle with some pepper to taste. Decorate with few thyme leaves before serving.

Nutrition information per serving: Kcal: 369, Protein: 21.7g, Carbs: 13.1g, Fats: 26.5g

56.   Red Pepper Beans

Ingredients:

1 ½ lb of beans, pre-cooked

2 medium-sized carrots, sliced

1 large red pepper, chopped

2 medium-sized onions, sliced

5 garlic cloves, minced

3 small tomatoes, sliced

1 cup of tomato sauce

1 small chili pepper, finely chopped

1 cup of celery, chopped

2 tbsp of olive oil

6 cups of water

Preparation:

With the cooker's lid off, heat the olive oil on high. Stir-fry the onions for 2 minutes, or until translucent.

Add carrots, pepper and garlic. Cook for about 10 minutes on medium-high temperature. Now, add the tomatoes, tomato sauce, and 1 cup of hot water.

Add the pre-cooked beans and 5 cups of water. Now add the celery and chili pepper.

Securely lock the cooker's lid. Set for 10 minutes on high.

Nutrition information per serving: Kcal: 356, Protein: 9.2g, Carbs: 49.4g, Fats: 6.3g

57. Moroccan Risotto

Ingredients:

1 cup of brown rice, pre-cooked

2 tbsp of extra-virgin olive oil

2 medium-sized carrots, grated

1 small tomato, peeled and finely chopped

1 tbsp Moroccan spice seasoning

1 medium-sized onion, peeled and chopped

6-7 dried apricots, halved

Preparation:

In a deep pot, bring 3 cups of water to a boiling point. Add rice and reduce the heat to a low temperature. Cook until all the water evaporates. Remove from the heat.

Preheat the oil in a frying pan over a medium-high temperature. Add onion and stir-fry until translucent.

Now, add tomato, apricots, and Moroccan spice seasoning.

Cook for another 5 minutes and then add rice. Stir well to combine.

Top with grated carrots and serve.

Nutrition information per serving: Kcal: 435, Protein: 15.9g, Carbs: 67.3g, Fats: 6.3g

JUICE RECIPES

1. Broccoli Cauliflower Juice

Ingredients:

1 cup broccoli, chopped

1 cup cauliflower, chopped

1 small Granny Smith's apple, cored

1 cup fresh kale, torn

¼ tsp ginger, ground

Preparation:

Wash the broccoli thoroughly and chop into small pieces. Set aside.

Wash the cauliflower and trim off the outer leaves. Cut into small pieces and set aside.

Wash the apple and cut lengthwise in half. Remove the core and cut into bite-sized pieces. Set aside.

Rinse the kale under cold running water and slightly drain. Torn with hands and set aside.

Now, combine broccoli, cauliflower, apple, and kale in a juicer and process until well juiced. Transfer to a serving glass and stir in the ground ginger.

Refrigerate for 10-15 minutes before serving.

Nutritional information per serving: Kcal: 131, Protein: 8.1g, Carbs: 36.8g, Fats: 1.5g

2. Apple Carrot Juice

Ingredients:

1 large Zestar apple, cored

1 medium-sized carrot, chopped

1 whole lemon, peeled

1 large peach, pitted

¼ tsp cinnamon, ground

2 oz water

Preparation:

Wash the apple and cut lengthwise in half. Remove the core and cut into bite-sized pieces. Set aside.

Wash and peel the carrot. Cut into small chunks and set aside.

Peel the lemon and cut lengthwise in half. Set aside.

Wash the peach and cut in half. Remove the pit and cut into bite-sized pieces. Set aside.

Now, combine apple, carrot lemon, and peach in a juicer. Process until nicely juiced. Transfer to a serving glass and stir in the water and cinnamon.

Add a few ice cubes and serve immediately.

Enjoy!

Nutritional information per serving: Kcal: 165, Protein: 3.6g, Carbs: 50.7g, Fats: 1.1g

3. Orange Raspberry Juice

Ingredients:

1 large orange, wedged

1 cup raspberries

2 large carrots, peeled and chopped

¼ tsp ginger, ground

1 tbsp liquid honey

Preparation:

Peel the orange and divide into wedges. Set aside.

Using a colander, rinse the raspberries under cold running water and drain. Set aside.

Wash the carrots and peel them. Cut into small chunks and set aside.

Now, combine orange, raspberries, and carrots in a juicer and process until well juiced. Transfer to a serving glass and stir in the ginger and honey.

Let it chill in the refrigerator for a while before serving.

Nutritional information per serving: Kcal: 204, Protein: 4.5g, Carbs: 67.1g, Fats: 1.3g

4. Beet Broccoli Juice

Ingredients:

1 whole beet, chopped

1 cup broccoli, chopped

1 cup purple cabbage, torn

1 cup Swiss chard, torn

1 cup cucumber, sliced

¼ tsp turmeric, ground

Preparation:

Wash the beets and trim off the green parts. Cut into bite-sized pieces and set aside.

Wash the broccoli and trim off the outer layers. Chop it into small pieces and set aside.

Combine purple cabbage and Swiss chard in a large colander. Wash thoroughly under cold running water and slightly drain. Torn with hands and set aside.

Wash the cucumber and cut into thin slices. Fill the measuring cup and reserve the rest for later. Set aside.

Now, combine beet, broccoli, purple cabbage, Swiss chard,

and cucumber in a juicer and process until juiced.

Transfer to a serving glass and stir in the turmeric. Refrigerate for 10 minutes and serve.

Enjoy!

Nutrition information per serving: Kcal: 79, Protein: 6.2g, Carbs: 23.7g, Fats: 0.8g

5. Cucumber Agave Juice

Ingredients:

1 cup cucumber, sliced

1 tsp agave nectar

1 cup cauliflower, chopped

1 cup fresh kale, chopped

1 whole lime, peeled

Preparation:

Wash the cucumber and cut into thin slices. Fill the measuring cup and reserve the rest for some other juice. Set aside.

Wash the kale thoroughly under cold running water and slightly drain. Chop into small pieces and set aside.

Peel the lime and cut lengthwise in half. Set aside.

Trim off the outer layer of the cauliflower. Cut into bite-sized pieces and wash it. Fill the measuring cup and sprinkle with some salt. Set aside.

Now, combine cucumber, kale, lime, and cauliflower in a juicer. Process until well juiced. Transfer to a serving glass and stir in the agave nectar.

Refrigerate before serving.

Enjoy!

Nutrition information per serving: Kcal: 107, Protein: 11.4g, Carbs: 30.4g, Fats: 1.8g

6. Lemon Apple Juice

Ingredients:

1 whole lemon, peeled

1 medium-sized Zestar apple, cored

1 cup raspberries

1 cup fresh mint, torn

1 cup cranberries

¼ tsp cinnamon, ground

Preparation:

Peel the lemon and cut lengthwise in half. Set aside.

Wash the apple and cut in half. Remove the core and cut into bite-sized pieces.

Combine raspberries and cranberries in a large colander. Rinse thoroughly under cold running water and slightly drain. Set aside.

Rinse the mint and torn with hands. Set aside.

Now, combine lemon, apple, raspberries, mint, and cranberries in a juicer and process until juiced. Transfer to a serving glass and stir in the cinnamon. Add some ice before serving.

Enjoy!

Nutrition information per serving: Kcal: 143, Protein: 3.8g, Carbs: 53.5g, Fats: 1.5g

7. Avocado Lemon Juice

Ingredients:

1 cup avocado, cubed

1 whole lemon, peeled

2 whole plums, chopped

1 medium-sized Granny Smith's apple, cored

¼ tsp cinnamon, ground

1 tbsp coconut water

Preparation:

Peel the avocado and cut in half. Remove the pit and cut into small cubes. Fill the measuring cup and reserve the rest for later.

Peel the lemon and cut into half. Set aside.

Wash the plums and cut lengthwise in half. Remove the pits and cut into bite-sized pieces. Set aside.

Wash the apple and cut in half. Remove the pit and cut into small pieces. Set aside.

Now, combine avocado, lemon plums, and apple in a juicer and process until juiced. Transfer to a serving glass and stir in the cinnamon and coconut water.

Refrigerate for 15 minutes before serving.

Enjoy!

Nutrition information per serving: Kcal: 341, Protein: 5.3g, Carbs: 56.1g, Fats: 22.8g

8. Lemon Strawberry Juice

Ingredients:

1 medium-sized pear, chopped

1 cup blueberries

1 whole lemon, peeled

½ cup strawberries, sliced

1 small ginger knob, peeled

1 oz water

Preparation:

Peel the lemon and cut in half. Set aside.

Wash the strawberries and remove the stems. Cut into small pieces and fill the measuring cup. Set aside.

Wash the pear and cut in half. Remove the core and cut into small pieces. Set aside.

Rinse the blueberries and fill the measuring cup. Set aside.

Peel the ginger knob and set aside.

Now, combine lemon, strawberries, pear, blueberries, and ginger in a juicer and process until juiced. Transfer to a serving glass and stir in the water.

Serve immediately.

Nutritional information per serving: Kcal: 143, Protein: 2.4g, Carbs: 52.7g, Fats: 0.8g

9. Cinnamon Watermelon Juice

Ingredients:

¼ tsp cinnamon, ground

1 medium-sized watermelon wedge

1 large banana, peeled

1 whole lime, peeled

1 small Granny Smith's apple, cored

Preparation:

Cut one large watermelon wedge and peel it. Remove the seeds and cut into bite-sized pieces. Wrap the rest of the melon in a plastic foil and refrigerate. Peel the banana and chop into small chunks. Set aside. Peel the lime and cut lengthwise in half. Set aside. Wash the apple and cut in half. Remove the core and cut into bite-sized pieces. Set aside.

Now, combine watermelon, lime, banana, and apple in a juicer and process until juiced. Transfer to a serving glass and stir in the cinnamon. Refrigerate for 10 minutes before serving.

Nutritional information per serving: Kcal: 226, Protein: 4.6g, Carbs: 29.4g, Fats: 1.2g

10. Lemon Artichoke Juice

Ingredients:

1 whole lemon, peeled

1 medium-sized artichoke, chopped

1 large blood orange, peeled

1 whole lime, peeled

1 tbsp liquid honey

1 oz water

Preparation:

Peel the lemon and lime. Cut each fruit lengthwise in half and set aside.

Trim off the outer layers of the artichoke using a sharp paring knife. Cut into bite-sized pieces and set aside.

Peel the orange and divide into wedges. Cut each wedge in half and set aside.

Now, combine lemon, artichoke, orange, and lime in a juicer. Process until well juiced. Transfer to a serving glass and stir in the honey and water.

Refrigerate for 10 minutes before serving.

Nutrition information per serving: Kcal: 149, Protein: 5.9g, Carbs: 33.8g, Fats: 0.5g

11. Apple Vanilla Juice

Ingredients:

1 small Red Delicious apple, cored

¼ tsp vanilla extract

1 cup blueberries

1 whole grapefruit, peeled

1 cup avocado, cubed

Preparation:

Wash the apple and cut lengthwise in half. Remove the core and cut into bite-sized pieces. Set aside.

Place the blueberries in a colander. Rinse well under cold running water and drain. Set aside.

Peel the grapefruit and divide into wedges. Cut each wedge in half and set aside.

Peel the avocado and cut lengthwise in half. Remove the pit and cut into small cubes. Fill the measuring cup and reserve the rest in the refrigerator.

Now, combine apple, blueberries, grapefruit, and avocado in a juicer and process until juiced. Transfer to a serving glass and stir in the vanilla extract. Refrigerate for 10 minutes before serving.

Nutrition information per serving: Kcal: 436, Protein: 6.4g, Carbs: 69.5g, Fats: 23.2g

12. Banana Pineapple Juice

Ingredients:

1 large banana, chunked

1 cup pineapple, chunked

1 cup strawberries, chopped

1 whole lemon, peeled

1 tbsp fresh mint, finely chopped

Preparation:

Peel the banana and cut into small chunks. Set aside.

Cut the top of the pineapple using a sharp paring knife. Gently remove all hard skin and slice it into thin slices. Fill the measuring cup and reserve the rest for later.

Wash the strawberries and remove the stems. Chop into small pieces and fill the measuring cup. Reserve the rest in the refrigerator.

Peel the lemon and cut lengthwise in half. Set aside.

Now, combine banana, pineapple, strawberries, and lemon in a juicer. Process until juiced. Transfer to a serving glass and stir in the mint.

Add few ice cubes and serve immediately.

Nutrition information per serving: Kcal: 224, Protein: 4.1g, Carbs: 69.4g, Fats: 1.3g

13. Blueberry Coconut Juice

Ingredients:

2 cups blueberries

2 oz coconut water

1 large honeydew melon wedge, chopped

1 medium-sized Zestar apple, cored

1 tbsp mint, finely chopped

Preparation:

Place the blueberries in a large colander. Rinse well under cold running water and drain. Set aside.

Cut melon lengthwise in half. Scoop out the seeds and then wash. Cut one large wedge and peel it. Cut into small cubes and set aside.

Wash the apple and cut lengthwise in half. Remove the core and cut into bite-sized pieces. Set aside.

Now, combine blueberry, honeydew melon, apple in a juicer. Process until juiced.

Transfer to a serving glass and stir in the coconut water and mint. Add some crushed ice and serve immediately.

Nutrition information per serving: Kcal: 283, Protein: 3.7g, Carbs: 85.1g, Fats: 1.5g

14. Lime Cauliflower Juice

Ingredients:

1 large lime, peeled

1 cup cauliflower, chopped

3 large leeks, chopped

1 large zucchini, chopped

2 oz water

Preparation:

Peel the lime and cut lengthwise in half. Set aside.

Trim off the outer leaves of cauliflower. Wash it and cut into small pieces. Set aside.

Wash the leeks and cut into small pieces. Set aside.

Peel the zucchini and cut in half. Scrape out the seeds and cut into small chunks. Set aside.

Now, combine lime, cauliflower, leeks, and zucchini in a juicer. Process until well juiced and stir in the water. Refrigerate for 10 minutes before serving.

Enjoy!

Nutritional information per serving: Kcal: 241, Protein: 13.2g, Carbs: 64.7g, Fats: 2.6g

15. Apple Strawberry Juice

Ingredients:

1 large Red Delicious apple, cored

1 cup strawberries, chopped

2 large peaches, pitted

1 large lemon, peeled

1 large kiwi, peeled

1 large orange, peeled

2 oz water

Preparation:

Wash the apple and cut half. Remove the core and cut into bite-sized pieces. Set aside.

Wash the strawberries under cold running water. Remove the green parts and cut into bite-sized pieces. Set aside.

Wash the peaches and cut in half. Remove the pits and cut into small pieces. Set aside.

Peel the lemon and kiwi. Cut lengthwise in half and set aside.

Peel the orange and divide into wedges. Set aside.

Now, combine apple, strawberries, peaches, lemon, kiwi, and orange in a juicer and process until well juiced. Transfer to serving glasses and stir in the water. Add some ice and serve immediately.

Enjoy!

Nutritional information per serving: Kcal: 345, Protein: 7.8g, Carbs: 105g, Fats: 2.3g

16. Carrot Watercress Juice

Ingredients:

2 large carrots, sliced

1 cup watercress, torn

1 cup pineapple, chunked

1 large lime, peeled

1 small ginger knob, peeled

2 oz water

Preparation:

Wash and peel the carrots. Cut into thin slices and set aside.

Wash the watercress thoroughly under cold running water. Torn with hands and set aside.

Peel the pineapple and cut into small chunks. Set aside.

Peel the lime and cut lengthwise in half. Set aside.

Peel the ginger root knob and cut into small pieces. Set aside.

Now, combine carrots, watercress, pineapple, lemon, and

ginger in a juicer and process until well juiced.

Transfer to serving glasses and stir in water.

Add some ice and serve.

Nutritional information per serving: Kcal: 135, Protein: 3.3g, Carbs: 40.6g, Fats: 3.3g

17. Pomegranate Orange Juice

Ingredients:

1 cup pomegranate seeds

2 large oranges, peeled

2 large apricots, pitted

1 cup green grapes

1 large lemon, peeled

1 small ginger slice, peeled

Preparation:

Cut the top of the pomegranate fruit using a sharp knife. Slice down to each of the white membranes inside of the fruit. Pop the seeds into a measuring cup and set aside.

Peel the oranges and divide into wedges. Set aside.

Wash the apricots and cut in half. Remove the pits and cut into small pieces. Set aside.

Rinse the grapes and fill the measuring cup. Reserve the rest in the refrigerator.

Peel the lemon and cut lengthwise in half. Set aside.

Peel the ginger slice and set aside.

Now, combine pomegranate, oranges, grapes, apricots, lemon, and ginger in a juicer. Process until well juiced and transfer to serving glasses. Refrigerate for 10 minutes before serving.

Nutritional information per serving: Kcal: 294, Protein: 7.2g, Carbs: 88.9g, Fats: 2.3g

18. Mint Papaya Juice

Ingredients:

1 tbsp fresh mint, chopped

1 large papaya, peeled and chopped

1 large Red Delicious apple, cored

1 cup pomegranate seeds

2 oz water

Preparation:

Peel the papaya and cut lengthwise in half. Scoop out the black seeds and flesh using a spoon. Cut into small chunks and set aside.

Wash the apple and cut in half. Using a sharp knife, remove the core and cut into bite-sized pieces. Set aside.

Cut the top of the pomegranate fruit using a sharp knife. Slice down to each of the white membranes inside of the fruit. Pop the seeds into a measuring cup and set aside.

Now, combine mint, papaya, apple, and pomegranate in a juicer. Process until well juiced and transfer to serving glasses. Stir in the water and refrigerate before serving.

Nutritional information per serving: Kcal: 438, Protein: 6.1g, Carbs: 129g, Fats: 3.4g

19. Beet Mint Juice

Ingredients:

1 cup beets, chopped

1 cup fresh mint, torn

2 cups raspberries

1 large Red Delicious apple, cored

1 large lemon, peeled

3 oz water

Preparation:

Wash the beets and trim off the green ends. Cut into small pieces and fill the measuring cup. Reserve the greens for some other juice.

Wash the raspberries under cold running water using a colander. Drain and set aside.

Wash the apple and cut in half. Remove the core and cut into bite-sized pieces. Set aside.

Rinse the mint thoroughly under cold running water and torn with hands. Set aside.

Peel the lemon and cut lengthwise in half. Set aside.

Now, combine beets, mint, raspberries, apple, and lemon in a juicer. Process until well juiced. Stir in the water and refrigerate for 15 minutes before serving.

Enjoy!

Nutritional information per serving: Kcal: 218, Protein: 7.5g, Carbs: 76.4g, Fats: 2.5g

20. Pumpkin Swiss Chard Juice

Ingredients:

2 cups pumpkin, cubed

1 cup Swiss chard, torn

1 large Granny Smith's apple, cored

¼ tsp cinnamon, ground

1 large cucumber, sliced

2 oz water

Preparation:

Peel the pumpkin and cut in half. Scoop out the seeds using a spoon. Cut one large wedge and peel it. Cut into small cubes and fill the measuring cup. Reserve the rest for some other juice.

Wash the Swiss chard thoroughly under cold running water. Drain and torn with hands. Set aside.

Wash the apple and cut in half. Remove the core and cut into bite-sized pieces. Set aside.

Wash the cucumber and cut into thin slices. Set aside.

Now, combine pumpkin, Swiss chard, apple, and cucumber

in a juicer. Process until well juiced and stir in the water and nutmeg.

Refrigerate for 10 minutes before serving.

Nutritional information per serving: Kcal: 196, Protein: 5.8g, Carbs: 55.4g, Fats: 1.1g

21. Watermelon Mint Juice

Ingredients:

1 cup watermelon, cubed

1 cup fresh mint, torn

2 cups blueberries

1 whole lime, peeled

¼ tsp cayenne pepper, ground

1 oz water

Preparation:

Cut one large watermelon wedge. Using a sharp paring knife, peel and cut into small cubes. Remove the seeds and set aside.

Rinse the mint and roughly torn it with hands. Set aside.

Place the blueberries in a large colander. Rinse well under cold running water and set aside.

Peel the lime and cut lengthwise in half. Set aside.

Now, combine watermelon, mint, blueberries, and lime in a juicer. Process until juiced. Transfer to a serving glass and stir in the cayenne pepper and water.

Refrigerate for 5 minutes before serving.

Nutritional information per serving: Kcal: 198, Protein: 4.1g, Carbs: 58.7g, Fats: 1.4g

22. Cherry Lemon Juice

Ingredients:

1 cup cherries, pitted

1 whole lemon, peeled

1 cup pineapple, chunked

1 cup spinach, chopped

¼ tsp cinnamon, ground

1 oz water

Preparation:

Place the cherries in a medium colander. Rinse well under cold running water and remove the stems, if any. Cut each in half and remove the pits. Fill the measuring cup and reserve the rest in the refrigerator.

Peel the lemon and cut lengthwise in half. Set aside.

Using a sharp paring knife, cut the top of the pineapple. Gently remove all hard skin and slice it into thin slices. Fill the measuring cup and reserve the rest for later.

Rinse the spinach thoroughly under cold running water. Drain and chop into small pieces. Set aside.

Now, combine cherries, lemon pineapple, and spinach in a juicer and process until juiced. Transfer to a serving glass and stir in the water.

Add some crushed ice and serve immediately.

Nutrition information per serving: Kcal: 196, Protein: 9.2g, Carbs: 59.3g, Fats: 1.5g

23. Apricot Honey Juice

Ingredients:

1 cup of apricots, pitted and halved

1 tbsp liquid honey

1 small pear, chopped

1 whole lemon, peeled and halved

1 small Granny Smith's apple, cored

1 cup fresh mint, torn

Preparation:

Wash the apricots and cut each lengthwise in half. Remove the pits and fill the measuring cup. Reserve the rest in the refrigerator for some other juice.

Wash the pear and cut in half. Remove the core and cut into small pieces. Set aside.

Peel the lemon and cut lengthwise in half. Set aside.

Wash the apple and cut lengthwise in half. Remove the core and chop into bite-sized pieces. Set aside.

Rinse the mint thoroughly under cold running water. Drain and torn into small pieces. Set aside.

Now, combine apricots, apple, pear, lemon, and mint in a juicer and process until well juiced. Transfer to a serving glass and add some ice before serving.

Enjoy!

Nutrition information per serving: Kcal: 217, Protein: 4.9g, Carbs: 68.5g, Fats: 1.5g

24. Celery Ginger Juice

Ingredients:

1 cup celery, chopped

1 whole kiwi, peeled

1 medium-sized Golden Delicious apple, cored

1 medium-sized orange, peeled

1 tbsp liquid honey

¼ tsp ginger, ground

Preparation:

Wash the celery and chop into small pieces. Fill the measuring cup and reserve the rest for later. Set aside.

Peel the kiwi and cut lengthwise in half. Set aside.

Wash the apple and cut lengthwise in half. Remove the core and cut into bite-sized pieces. Set aside.

Peel the orange and divide into wedges. Cut each wedge in half and set aside.

Now, combine kiwi, apple, celery, and orange in a juicer and process until juiced. Transfer to a serving glass and stir in the honey and ginger.

Refrigerate for 15 minutes before serving.

Enjoy!

Nutrition information per serving: Kcal: 172, Protein: 3.5g, Carbs: 51.2g, Fats: 1.1g

25. Apricot Orange Juice

Ingredients:

1 large apricot, pitted

1 large orange, wedged

1 cup pomegranate seeds

1 large lemon, peeled

1 large carrot, sliced

2 oz coconut water

Preparation:

Wash the apricot and cut in half. Remove the pit and cut into small pieces. Set aside.

Peel the orange and divide into wedges. Set aside.

Cut the top of the pomegranate fruit using a sharp knife. Slice down to each of the white membranes inside of the fruit. Pop the seeds into measuring cup and set aside.

Peel the lemon and cut lengthwise in half. Set aside.

Peel and wash the carrot. Cut into thin slices and set aside.

Now, combine apricot, orange, pomegranate seeds, lemon,

and carrot in a juicer. Process until well juiced and transfer to serving glasses. Stir in the coconut water and add few ice cubes before serving.

Nutritional information per serving: Kcal: 241, Protein: 7.3g, Carbs: 73.9g, Fats: 2.3g

26. Orange Pineapple Juice

Ingredients:

1 large orange, peeled

1 cup pineapple, chunked

1 whole grapefruit, peeled

1 cup cauliflower, chopped

¼ cup pure coconut water, unsweetened

Preparation:

Peel the orange and grapefruit and divide into wedges. Set aside.

Cut the top of a pineapple and peel it using a sharp knife. Cut into small chunks. Reserve the rest of the pineapple in a refrigerator.

Trim off the outer leaves of cauliflower. Wash it and cut into small pieces. Reserve the rest in the refrigerator.

Now, combine orange, pineapple, grapefruit, and cauliflower in a juicer and process until juiced. Transfer to serving glasses and stir in the pure coconut water.

Add few ice cubes and serve immediately.

Nutritional information per serving: Kcal: 247, Protein: 6.5g, Carbs: 74g, Fats: 1g

27. Cantaloupe Orange Juice

Ingredients:

1 cup cantaloupe, chopped

1 large orange, peeled

1 cup blackberries

1 cup fresh mint, torn

¼ tsp cinnamon, ground

Preparation:

Cut the cantaloupe in half. Scrape out the seeds and cut one large wedge. Peel and chop into small pieces. Fill the measuring cup and wrap the rest in a plastic foil. Refrigerate for later.

Peel the orange and divide into wedges. Cut each wedge in half and set aside.

Place the blackberries in a colander and rinse well. Drain and set aside.

Rinse the mint under cold running water and drain. Torn into small pieces and set aside.

Now, combine cantaloupe, orange blackberries, and mint

in a juicer and process until juiced. Transfer to a serving glass and stir in the cinnamon. Optionally, add some water to increase the juice amount.

Serve immediately.

Nutrition information per serving: Kcal: 157, Protein: 5.9g, Carbs: 51.9g, Fats: 1.5g

28. Cucumber Apple Juice

Ingredients:

1 medium-sized cucumber, chopped

1 small Golden Delicious apple, cored

1 large honeydew melon wedge, chopped

1 cup fresh mint, chopped

1 oz coconut water

Preparation:

Wash the cucumber and cut into thin slices. Set aside.

Wash the apple and cut lengthwise in half. Remove the core and cut into bite-sized pieces. Set aside.

Cut the melon in half. Cut one large wedge and peel the peel it. Cut into small pieces and set aside. Wrap the rest of the melon in a plastic foil and refrigerate for later.

Place mint in a colander and wash thoroughly. Slightly drain and chop into small pieces. Set aside.

Now, combine cucumber, apple, melon, and mint in a juicer and process until juiced.

Transfer to a serving glass and stir in the water. Optionally, add 1 tablespoon of lemon juice for a better taste. Refrigerate for 10 minutes before serving.

Enjoy!

Nutrition information per serving: Kcal: 139, Protein: 4.1g, Carbs: 40.5g, Fats: 0.9g

29. Watermelon Celery Juice

Ingredients:

1 medium-sized watermelon slice

1 cup celery, chopped

2 cups cherries, pitted

1 small ginger knob, peeled

1 oz water

Preparation:

Cut the watermelon in half. Cut one medium-sized wedge and wrap the rest in a plastic foil and refrigerate. Dice the wedge and remove the pits. Set aside.

Wash the celery and cut into small pieces. Fill the measuring cup and reserve the rest for later. Set aside.

Rinse the cherries under cold running water using a colander. Drain and cut each in half. Remove the pits and set aside.

Peel the ginger knob and cut into small pieces. Set aside.

Now, combine watermelon, celery, cherries, and ginger knob in a juicer and process until juiced. Transfer to a serving glass and stir in the water. Optionally, you can use coconut water if you like.

Serve immediately.

Nutrition information per serving: Kcal: 143, Protein: 3.4g, Carbs: 40.2g, Fats: 0.7g

30. Apple Carrot Juice

Ingredients:

3 medium-sized carrots, sliced

1 cup parsnips, sliced

2 large Gala apples, peeled and cored

¼ cup water

1 tbsp fresh lemon juice

Preparation:

Wash the carrots and parsnips and cut into thick slices. Set aside.

Wash the apples and remove the core. Cut into bite-sized pieces and set aside.

Now, combine apples, carrots, and parsnips in a juicer and process until juiced.

Transfer to serving glasses and stir in the water and lemon juice. Garnish with some mint and refrigerate before serving.

Enjoy!

Nutritional information per serving: Kcal: 332, Protein: 5.4g, Carbs: 100g, Fats: 1.6g

31. Cabbage Grapefruit Juice

Ingredients:

2 whole kiwis, peeled

1 cup carrots, chopped

2 cups green cabbage, shredded

1 whole grapefruit, peeled

1 tbsp honey, raw

Preparation:

Wash the cabbage thoroughly and roughly chop it using hands. Set aside.

Wash the grapefruit and cut into chunks. Set aside.

Wash the carrots and cut into small pieces. Set aside.

Peel the kiwis and cut in half. Set aside.

Now, process cabbage, grapefruit, carrots, and kiwis in a juicer. Transfer to a serving glass and stir in the honey.

Serve immediately.

Nutritional information per serving: Kcal: 219, Protein: 6.9g, Carbs: 69g, Fats: 1.5g

32. Cantaloupe Kale Juice

Ingredients:

1 cup cantaloupe, cubed

1 cup fresh kale, torn

1 small Red Delicious apple, cored

1 cup beets, sliced

¼ tsp ginger, ground

Preparation:

Cut the cantaloupe in half. Scrape out the seeds and cut one large wedge. Peel and chop into small pieces. Fill the measuring cup and wrap the rest in a plastic foil. Refrigerate for later.

Rinse the kale thoroughly under cold running water. Drain and torn into small pieces. Set aside.

Wash the apple and cut lengthwise in half. Remove the core and cut into bite-sized pieces. Set aside.

Wash the beets and trim off the green ends. Cut into thin slices and fill the measuring cup. Reserve the rest for some other juice.

Now, combine cantaloupe, kale, apple, and beets in a juicer and process until juiced. Transfer to a serving glass and stir in the ginger.

Add some ice and serve immediately.

Nutrition information per serving: Kcal: 181, Protein: 7g, Carbs: 51.1g, Fats: 1.4g

33. Carrot Apple Juice

Ingredients:

1 cup mango, chunked

1 medium-sized orange, wedged

1 large carrot, sliced

1 small Granny Smith's apple, cored and chopped

1 oz coconut water

Preparation:

Peel the mango and cut into chunks. Fill the measuring cup and reserve the rest for later.

Peel the orange and divide into wedges. Set aside.

Wash and peel the carrot. Cut into bite-sized pieces and set aside.

Wash the apple and cut in half. Remove the core and cut into bite-sized pieces. Set aside.

Now, combine mango, orange, carrot, and apple in a juicer and process until juiced. Transfer to a serving glass and stir in the coconut water.

Serve immediately and enjoy!

Nutrition information per serving: Kcal: 189, Protein: 2.6g, Carbs: 56.4g, Fats:1.1g

34. Lime Melon Juice

Ingredients:

1 large lime, peeled

2 large honeydew melon wedges

1 cup avocado, peeled and pitted

5 tbsp fresh mint

1 medium-sized pineapple slice, chopped

Preparation:

Peel the lime and cut lengthwise in half. Set aside.

Cut the honeydew melon lengthwise in half. Scoop out the seeds using a spoon. Cut the large wedges and peel them. Cut into small chunks and place in a bowl. Wrap the rest of the melon in a plastic foil and refrigerate.

Peel the avocado and cut in half. Remove the pit and cut into chunks. Add it to the bowl with melon and set aside.

Wash the mint leaves and soak in water for 5 minutes.

Now, process lime, honeydew melon, avocado, mint, and pineapple in a juicer. Transfer to serving glasses and serve immediately.

Enjoy!

Nutritional information per serving: Kcal: 321, Protein: 5.2g, Carbs: 46.8g, Fats: 22.6g

35. Pomegranate Kale Juice

Ingredients:

½ cup pomegranate seeds

½ cup fresh kale, torn

1 tsp fresh ginger, freshly grated

1 large Granny Smith's apple, cored

1 tbsp agave nectar

Preparation:

Cut the top of the pomegranate fruit using a sharp knife. slice down to each of the white membranes inside of the fruit. Pop the seeds into a medium-sized bowl.

Rinse the kale thoroughly. Drain and torn into small pieces. Set aside.

Peel and grate the ginger knob. Fill up the measuring teaspoon and reserve the rest in the refrigerator.

Wash the apple and remove the core. Cut into bite-sized pieces and set aside.

Process the pomegranate seeds, kale, and apple in a juicer until well juiced.

Transfer to serving glasses and stir in the ginger. Add some water to adjust the thickness and stir in the agave nectar.

Serve immediately.

Nutrition information per serving: Kcal: 194, Protein: 6.2g, Carbs: 54.2g, Fats: 2.4g

36. Spinach Avocado Juice

Ingredients:

1 cup fresh spinach, torn

1 cup avocado, cubed

1 cup artichoke, chopped

1 cup green cabbage, torn

¼ tsp ginger powder

Preparation:

Combine spinach and cabbage in a large colander. Wash thoroughly under cold running water. Drain and torn into small pieces. Set aside.

Peel the avocado and cut lengthwise in half. Remove the pit and cut into small cubes. Fill the measuring cup and reserve the rest in the refrigerator.

Trim off the outer layers of the artichoke using a sharp paring knife. Cut into bite-sized pieces and fill the measuring cup. Reserve the rest for later.

Now, combine spinach, avocado, artichoke, and cabbage in a juicer and process until juiced. Transfer to a serving glass and stir in the ginger powder.

Refrigerate for 15 minutes before serving.

Nutrition information per serving: Kcal: 282, Protein: 15.4g, Carbs: 42.6g, Fats: 23.2g

37. Cantaloupe Mint Juice

Ingredients:

1 cup cantaloupe, chopped

1 cup fresh mint, torn

1 whole plum, chopped

1 large orange, peeled

¼ tsp ginger, ground

Preparation:

Cut the cantaloupe in half. Scoop out the seeds and flesh. Cut and peel one large wedge. Chop into chunks and fill the measuring cup. Reserve the rest of the cantaloupe in a refrigerator.

Wash the mint thoroughly under cold running water. Torn into small pieces and set aside.

Peel the orange and divide into wedges. Cut each wedge in half and set aside.

Wash the plum and cut in half. Remove the pit and chop into small pieces. Set aside.

Now, combine cantaloupe, mint, plum, and orange in a

juicer and process until juiced. Transfer to a serving glass and stir in the ginger.

Serve immediately.

Nutrition information per serving: Kcal: 151, Protein: 4.4g, Carbs: 45.6g, Fats: 0.9g

38. Pomegranate Plum Juice

Ingredients:

1 cup pomegranate seeds

3 whole plums, pitted and chopped

1 cup yellow pumpkin, cubed

1 medium-sized orange, peeled

¼ tsp ginger, ground

1 oz water

Preparation:

Cut the top of the pomegranate fruit using a sharp paring knife. Slice down to each of the white membranes inside of the fruit. Pop the seeds into a measuring cup and set aside.

Wash the plums and cut into halves. Remove the pits and chop into small pieces. Set aside.

Cut the top of a pumpkin. Cut lengthwise in half and then scrape out the seeds. Cut one large wedge and peel it. Cut into small cubes and fill the measuring cup. Reserve the rest in the refrigerator.

Peel the orange and divide into wedges. Cut each wedge in

half and set aside.

Now, combine pomegranate, plums, pumpkin, and orange in a juicer. Process until juiced. Transfer to a serving glass and stir in the ginger and water.

Refrigerate for 15 minutes before serving.

Enjoy!

Nutrition information per serving: Kcal: 214, Protein: 5.2g, Carbs: 61.8g, Fats: 1.8g

39. Strawberry Grapefruit Juice

Ingredients:

2 large strawberries, chopped

2 large grapefruits, peeled

1 large Red Delicious apple, cored

1 small ginger knob, peeled

2 oz coconut water

Preparation:

Wash the strawberries and cut into small pieces. Set aside.

Peel the grapefruits and divide into wedges. Set aside.

Wash the apple and cut in half. Remove the core and cut into bite-sized pieces. Set aside.

Peel the ginger knob and set aside.

Now, combine strawberries, grapefruits, apple, and ginger in a juicer. Process until well juiced and transfer to serving glasses. Stir in the coconut water and refrigerate for 15 minutes, or add some ice before serving.

Nutritional information per serving: Kcal: 302, Protein: 4.8g, Carbs: 86.3g, Fats: 1.7g

40. Lime Zucchini Juice

Ingredients:

1 large lime, peeled

1 large zucchini, seeded

3 large kiwis, peeled

1 cup pomegranate seeds

1 large orange, peeled

Preparation:

Peel the lime and kiwi. Cut lengthwise in half and set aside.

Wash the zucchini and cut in half. Scoop out the seeds using a spoon. Cut into small chunks and set aside. Cut the top of the pomegranate fruit using a sharp knife. Slice down to each of the white membranes inside of the fruit. Pop the seeds into a measuring cup and set aside. Peel the orange and divide into wedges. Set aside. Now, process lime, zucchini, kiwi, pomegranate seeds, and orange in a juicer. Transfer to a serving glasses and add some ice cubes before serving.

Nutritional information per serving: Kcal: 183, Protein: 8.5g, Carbs: 52.6g, Fats: 1.6g

41. Guava Cucumber Juice

Ingredients:

1 cup guava, chopped

1 large cucumber, sliced

1 cup pineapple, chopped

2 large limes, peeled

1 tbsp fresh mint, chopped

2 oz water

Preparation:

Wash the guava and cut into chunks. Fill the measuring cup and reserve the rest for some other recipe in a refrigerator.

Wash the cucumber and cut into thin slices. Set aside.

Cut the top of a pineapple and peel it using a sharp knife. Cut into small chunks and fill the measuring cup. Reserve the rest of the pineapple in a refrigerator.

Peel the limes and cut lengthwise in half. Set aside.

Now, combine guava, cucumber, pineapple, limes, and mint in a juicer. Process until well juiced and transfer to serving glasses. Stir in the water and refrigerate for 15 minutes before serving.

Nutritional information per serving: Kcal: 158, Protein: 4.7g, Carbs: 47.9g, Fats: 1.1g

42. Cucumber Plum Juice

Ingredients:

1 large cucumber, sliced

5 large plums, pitted

1 cup blackberries

1 cup green cabbage, chopped

2 oz water

Preparation:

Wash the cucumber and cut into thin slices. Set aside.

Wash the plums and cut in half. Remove the pits and cut into quarters. Set aside.

Rinse the blackberries under cold running water using a colander. Slightly drain and set aside.

Wash the cabbage thoroughly under cold running water. Drain and roughly chop it. Set aside.

Now, combine cucumber, plums, blackberries, and cabbage in a juicer and process until juice. Transfer to serving glasses and stir in the water. Refrigerate for 10 minutes before serving.

Nutritional information per serving: Kcal: 221, Protein: 7.5g, Carbs: 69.1g, Fats: 2.1g

ADDITIONAL TITLES FROM THIS AUTHOR

70 Effective Meal Recipes to Prevent and Solve Being Overweight: Burn Fat Fast by Using Proper Dieting and Smart Nutrition

By Joe Correa CSN

48 Acne Solving Meal Recipes: The Fast and Natural Path to Fixing Your Acne Problems in Less Than 10 Days!

By Joe Correa CSN

41 Alzheimer's Preventing Meal Recipes: Reduce or Eliminate Your Alzheimer's Condition in 30 Days or Less!

By Joe Correa CSN

70 Effective Breast Cancer Meal Recipes: Prevent and Fight Breast Cancer with Smart Nutrition and Powerful Foods

By Joe Correa CSN

www.ingramcontent.com/pod-product-compliance
Lightning Source LLC
Chambersburg PA
CBHW052028070526
44584CB00016B/1943